The Lampstand Foundation:

It takes a Reformed

Criminal to reform Criminals

By
David H. Lukenbill

A Chulu Press Book

Chulu Press First Edition published 2014

IBSN: 978-0-9892429-2-9

Published by The Lampstand Foundation

We glorify God to attract others to Him

For Marlene & Erika Always

Contents

Chapter One

The Lampstand Foundation is a 501 c (3) nonprofit corporation founded by David H. Lukenbill in Sacramento, California in 2003 as a lay apostolate built on the social teaching of the Catholic Church, to provide leadership development tools for community & prison apostolates, managed by reformed criminals working to reform criminals.

Our Vision

Inspiring criminals who have transformed their lives, secured college degrees, and returned home to Rome; to show others the transformative path, and how the pain of suffering can become the power of teaching.

Our Mission

To transform the repentant criminal, suffering from his distance from God, into a deep knowledge leader who can teach other criminals the path to redemption through the Catholic Church.

Our Core Beliefs

Suffering transformed builds souls. Just as the muscle tissue tearing that leads to greater physical muscle growth resulting from body building, suffering is soul tearing which, through redemption, allows soul growth.

1) Deep knowledge leadership: college-educated, transformed criminals, professionally trained to manage criminal transformative organizations; will dramatically improve the effectiveness of criminal transformation.

2) Catholic social thought forms the intellectual and spiritual foundation of criminal transformation.

3) Grassroots criminal transformation organizations need ongoing access to capacity building services.

4) Business and professional leadership, working to create community social capital through the transformation of criminals, will benefit from gaining knowledge about Catholic social thought.

Our Goals

We want to facilitate the leadership development of penitential criminals whose personal transformation, education, and reconciliation or conversion to Catholicism has inspired them to seek graduate degrees, professional organizational training, social teaching training, and assume a leadership role in the community helping other criminals transform their lives.

1) To inspire educated and transformed criminals who are baptized Catholics and want to help others, gain a graduate college education and professional training.

2) To provide capacity building tools to criminal transforming organizations about Catholic social teaching, start-up planning, strategic planning, fund development, board development, communications & marketing, and for profit business development.

3) To educate the business and professional community about the leadership capability of educated, transformed criminals and the use of Catholic social teaching as a transformative tool.

Chapter Two

Our Apostolate Principles

1) We will defend innocent human life in all that we do.

"**80.** Reason attests that there are objects of the human act which are by their nature "incapable of being ordered" to God, because they radically contradict the good of the person made in his image. These are the acts which, in the Church's moral tradition, have been termed "intrinsically evil" (*intrinsece malum*): they are such *always and per se,* in other words, on account of their very object, and quite apart from the ulterior intentions of the one acting and the circumstances. Consequently, without in the least denying the influence on morality exercised by circumstances and especially by intentions, the Church teaches that "there exist acts which *per se* and in themselves, independently of circumstances, are always seriously wrong by reason of their object". The Second Vatican Council itself, in discussing the respect due to the human person, gives a number of examples of such acts. "Whatever is opposed to life itself, such as any type of murder, genocide, abortion, euthanasia, or wilful self-destruction, whatever violates the integrity of the human person, such as mutilation, torments inflicted on body or mind, attempts to coerce the will itself; whatever insults human dignity, such as subhuman living conditions, arbitrary imprisonment, deportation, slavery, prostitution, the selling of women and children; as well as disgraceful working conditions, where people are treated as mere instruments of gain rather than as free and responsible persons; all these things and others like them are infamies indeed. They poison human society, and they do more harm to those who practise them than to those who suffer from the injury. Moreover, they are a supreme dishonour to the Creator." (Pope John Paul II, 1993, *Veritatis Splendor* #80)

2) We will work for social justice in all that we do.

"**1928.** Society ensures social justice when it provides the conditions that allow associations or individuals to obtain what is their due, according to their nature and their vocation. Social justice is linked to the common good and the exercise of authority.

"**1929.** Social justice can be obtained only in respecting the transcendent dignity of man. The person represents the ultimate end of society, which is ordered to him:

"What is at stake is the dignity of the human person, whose defense and promotion have been entrusted to us by the Creator, and to whom the men and women at every moment of history are strictly and responsibly in debt.

"**1930.** Respect for the human person entails respect for the rights that flow from his dignity as a creature. These rights are prior to society and must be recognized by it. They are the basis of the moral legitimacy of every authority: by flouting them, or refusing to recognize them in its positive legislation, a society undermines its own moral legitimacy. If it does not respect them, authority can rely only on force or violence to obtain obedience from its subjects. It is the Church's role to remind men of good will of these rights and to distinguish them from unwarranted or false claims." (*Catechism of the Catholic Church,* #1928-1930)

3) We know that our work is with, and through, the community.

"In our time, *the role of human work* is becoming increasingly important as the productive factor both of non-material and of material wealth. Moreover, it is becoming clearer how a person's work is naturally interrelated with the work of others. More than ever, *work is work with others* and *work for others*: it is a matter of doing something for someone else." (Pope John Paul II, 1991, *Centesimus Annus,* #31)

4) We know that Catholic social thought is a transformative social force.

"**2419** "Christian revelation...promotes deeper understanding of the laws of social living." The Church receives from the Gospel the full revelation of the truth about man. When she fulfills her mission of proclaiming the Gospel, she bears witness to man, in the name of Christ, to his dignity and his vocation to the communion of persons. She teaches him the demands of justice and peace in conformity with divine wisdom.

"**2420** The Church makes a moral judgment about economic and social matters, "when the fundamental rights of the person or the salvation of souls requires it." In the moral order she bears a mission distinct from that of political authorities: The Church is concerned with the temporal aspects of the common good because they are ordered to the sovereign Good, our ultimate end. She strives to inspire right attitudes with respect to earthly goods and in socio-economic relationships.

"**2421** The social doctrine of the Church developed in the nineteenth century when the Gospel encountered modern industrial society with its new structures for the production of consumer goods, its new concept of society, the state and authority, and its new forms of labor and ownership. The development of the doctrine of the Church on economic and social matters attests the permanent value of the Church's teaching at the same time as it attests the true meaning of her Tradition, always living and active.

"**2422** The Church's social teaching comprises a body of doctrine, which is articulated as the Church interprets events in the course of history, with the assistance of the Holy Spirit, in the light of the whole of what has been revealed by Jesus Christ. This teaching can be more easily accepted by men of good will, the more the faithful let themselves be guided by it." (*Catechism of the Catholic Church* 2419-2422)

5) We know that corporal works of mercy are essential to comfort the suffering, and that spiritual works of mercy are essential to stop the suffering.

"**2447** The *works of mercy* are charitable actions by which we come to the aid of our neighbor in his spiritual and bodily necessities. Instructing, advising, consoling, comforting are spiritual works of mercy, as are forgiving and bearing wrongs patiently. The corporal works of mercy consist especially in feeding the hungry, sheltering the homeless, clothing the naked, visiting the sick and imprisoned, and burying the dead. Among all these, giving alms to the poor is one of the chief witnesses to fraternal charity: it is also a work of justice pleasing to God:

> He who has two coats, let him share with him who has none and he who has food must do likewise. But give for alms those things which are within; and behold, everything is clean for you. If a brother or sister is ill-clad and in lack of daily food, and one of you says to them, "Go in peace, be warmed and filled," without giving them the things needed for the body, what does it profit? (*Catechism of the Catholic Church* 2447)

Chapter Three

Our Criminal Justice Principles

1) *Broken windows policing works.* Allowing even the minor violation of a broken window in an area helps create the impression of an environment where law and order does not prevail and where crime flourishes. Responding quickly and efficiently to all crimes, regardless of the perceived state of seriousness or other local community concerns, is the foundation of good police work.

2) *The response to crime should be timely, balanced, and just.* When justice is for sale, either through wealth, influence, or ideology, a fertile soil is created from which crime grows. The training and education of professionals in the criminal justice system is built on a foundation of traditional and well-reasoned concepts of justice and it needs continual reinforcement to remain an effective response to crime.

3) *Prison is an appropriate criminal sanction to protect society and punish the criminal, while allowing the opportunity for criminal reformation.* Prison is an effective sanction for crime which has been used by human beings since ancient times. It serves to protect the public from predatory crime, acts as a deterrence and as incapacitation, and allows the penitential criminal the opportunity—while removed from the community—to reflect upon and correct his criminal behavior.

4) *Capital punishment is an appropriate response to the criminal evil of murder, rape, and pedophilia.* Capital punishment is often the only effective social method available to protect the innocent and applied with dispatch after legal review of the crimes charged and determining the fitness of its application, should be considered an appropriate sentence for murderers, rapists and pedophiles; who, knowing the time of their death, are able, with certainty of their remaining time to do so, seek God's forgiveness. Lane (2010) notes: "During the decade beginning in 1997, five states enacted the death penalty for rape of a child--though the Supreme Court struck those laws down in 2008." Lane, C. (2010). *Stay of execution: Saving the death penalty from itself.* New York: Rowman & Littlefield Publishers. (p. 66)

5) *Repentant criminals deserve a second chance.* Excepting those cases of serious predatory behavior deserving the death penalty or natural life in prison, repentant criminals, once they have clearly shown—over a ten year period after being released from criminal justice supervision—that they have transformed their life by becoming a productive member of their family, their church, their work, and their community, should be allowed to apply for a complete pardon in a simple straightforward process.

6) *It takes a reformed criminal to reform criminals.* For generations the ability of non-criminals— even those with the highest professional and academic credentials—to effectively rehabilitate criminals has proven, based on sound evaluations, to be virtually non-existent. Recruiting reformed criminals who have, through education, training, and the development of a deep knowledge leadership approach to criminal transformation, may well succeed where others have failed. Considering the current recidivism rate of 70-80%, and with the consensus that peer-based help does, at the very least, attract those who want help to transformative programs, it is time to try this approach in a substantial enough way, over time and properly evaluated, to discover if we can rely on it as a valuable tool for large-scale implementation.

7) In the work of criminal reformation, it is vital to keep in mind that the criminal—not society, capitalism, or the criminal justice system—is the problem. Some criminal justice advocates take the position that among the people connected with the carceral world, the good guys are the criminals and the police, district attorneys, prison guards, and the legislators who support stringent criminal sanctions, are the bad guys.

This is the absolutely wrong position, for in virtually any carceral population in America it is the criminals who are the indisputable bad guys, while the good guys are the ones protecting the public from the depredations of criminals. Those who parlay the myths of Hollywood or Marxism into an intellectual stance that fails to understand this basic fact, does everyone a disservice—in particular the penitential criminal—who may find little reason for proper expiation within a culture defining criminality as somehow admirable.

Chapter Four

Our Program

Lampstand's direct teaching work is supplemented by a monthly e-letter, quarterly newsletter, an annual policy primer research report released on the feast day of St. Dismas on March 25th, an annual book from Chulu Press (a Lampstand imprint), and periodic monographs.

Our Publications

Annual Books

***The Criminal's Search for God: Criminal Transformation, Catholic Social Teaching, Deep Knowledge Leadership, and Communal Reentry*, by David H. Lukenbill (2006)** This book is about a criminal life, personal transformation through education and deep spiritual work, the principles of Catholic social teaching, and the type of leadership needed to develop and manage effective criminal transformation programs. **Paperback & E-Book, Free to members, or the paperback can be ordered through Amazon.**

***Carceral World, Communal City*, by David H. Lukenbill (2007)** "The criminal world in the United States, with the carceral shaping of it, has become a coherent entity and within that entity it is the criminal world leadership to whom we must look for transformative leadership who have already transformed the pain of their suffering into the power of teaching others." (p. 8). **Paperback & E-Book, Free to members, or the paperback can be ordered through Amazon.**

The Criminal, The Cross & The Church: The Interior Journey, **by David H. Lukenbill (2008)** "The penitential criminal working to reform other criminals, wisely spends the rest of his life atoning for the harm he has done during his criminal life; not because the world requires it, but because the eternal balance requires it, his immortal soul requires it, and God wishes it." (Frontpiece) **Paperback & E-Book, Free to members, or the paperback can be ordered through Amazon.**

Capital Punishment & Catholic Social Teaching: A Tradition of Support, **by David H. Lukenbill (2009)** "This book is a defense of the scriptural and traditional Catholic position of support for capital punishment as expressed in the two universal catechisms, the *Catechism of the Council of Trent,* published by Pope Pius V in 1566, and the *Catechism of the Catholic Church,* published by Pope John Paul II in 1992 & 1997 (First and Second Edition), in response to calls for its abolition." (p. 9) Paperback or E-Book is free to members, or the paperback can be ordered through Amazon.

Invictus: The Way of the Apostolate, **by David H. Lukenbill (2010)** "This book is for penitential professional criminals whose involvement in the criminal/carceral world is of long duration and commitment. Professional criminals commit crimes for money and live by the ancient criminal way that precludes betrayal of partners or hurting women and children. To professional criminals, crime is their profession and way of life. To those professional criminals who are very good—and lucky—at what they do and never get caught, my work will have little value. It is for those professional criminals who do get caught and serve time in prison, comprising approximately 70 – 80% of the prison population; and who, at some point, may enter a penitential state." (pp. 11-12) Paperback or E-Book is free to members, or the paperback can be ordered through Amazon.

The Lampstand Prison Ministry: Constructed On Catholic Social Teaching & the History of the Catholic Church, by David H. Lukenbill (2011) "The foundational ideas animating the Lampstand prison ministry—that it takes a reformed criminal to reform criminals and that the conversion approach must be intellectual—are ideas I have been working with since the beginning of my reformation from criminality at age thirty five, as I began seeing the world from the perspective of a college education (leading to a successful criminal rehabilitative college-based educational program I developed and managed) and continuing to the final washing from my spirit the last remnants of a lifetime of criminal thinking twenty years later, in the waters of baptism. The peer relationship is where the impact this apostolate may have on future criminal activity lies, and it will be seen most dramatically within the Lampstand prison ministry where the apostolate work will *only* be optimized by conversions of the criminal/carceral elite— the professional criminal—whose history within rehabilitative work is virtually nil, because for him, the rewards of deep immersion within the criminal/carceral culture are too great, and other than as a ruse, rehabilitation is considered a tragic fool's errand." (p. 11)

Paperback or E-Book is free to members, or the paperback can be ordered through Amazon.

The Criminal's Search for God: Sources, **by David H. Lukenbill (2012)** "This book is a reflection on the collection of ideas within a group of books—sources—that played such a large role in the development of my thinking; initially to deepen my criminality, but eventually becoming the soil from which my transformation and conversion to Catholicism grew. Most of my exploration of the ideas in these books occurred in prison or shortly after release and as such, they were works from which I drew ideas that largely supported and expanded the underlying narrative of the criminal/carceral world within which I lived, and are largely congruent with its driving ethos. When I was in prison I read whatever books were available in the prison library or those I could get mailed in with my very limited budget. (p. 9) Paperback or E-Book is free to members, or the paperback can be ordered through Amazon.

Catholicism, Communism & Criminal Reformation, **by David H. Lukenbill (2013)** "What is important—in the context of our apostolate work through The Lampstand Foundation—is not the theory of Communism, "to each according to need", which many may support; but the influence on criminals from the system of government and its practice under Lenin and Stalin in Russia, Mao in China, and the lessor monsters of our world; practice continuing largely unchanged today except as modified within the constrictions created by the ability of global communications about governmental atrocities making it much more difficult to keep such atrocities hidden now than during the last century; and a governing practice diametrically opposed to the sacred doctrine of the Catholic Church, who Communism sees as its most dangerous enemy." (p. 13) Paperback or E-Book is free to members, or the paperback can be ordered through Amazon.

Annual Papers

St. Dismas Day Policy Primer #1: Terms-Thesis-Policy, (March 25, 2007) E-Report (Free to members only)

Summary: A criminal, as we use the term, is a professional criminal. Our thesis is that it takes a reformed criminal to reform criminals, and the policy we suggest is that of providing financial support for a model reentry program managed by a reformed criminal.

St. Dismas Day Policy Primer #2: Catholic Social Teaching & Capital Punishment: A Tradition of Support, (March 25, 2008) E-Report (Free to members only)

Summary: One of the strongest statements from Christ concerning capital punishment is Matthew 18:6. The magisterium of the Catholic Church supports the use of capital punishment. Those within the social science field informed by Catholic teaching, with professional knowledge of criminal justice issues and an understanding of how evil is expressed within the criminal world, embrace that tradition. Research clearly indicates that capital punishment deters crime and saves lives.

St. Dismas Day Policy Primer #3: Justice, Theology, Criminal Transformation & Pope Pius

XII, (March 25, 2009) E-Report (Free to members only)

Summary: Justice informed by the theology of the Church, expressed through the social teaching, and responding to the call of Pope Pius XII, can transform criminals. These stated principles, when coupled with the work of the Church through its saints, through its Popes, and the entire history of two thousand years of standing against the gates of hell, is a concrete story of standing on principle, speaking truth to power, walking the talk, proclaiming the truth to man; that will resonate with the criminal—when presented by another who shares the depth of experience represented by the criminal/carceral world—like none other.

St. Dismas Day Policy Primer #4: Unpacking the Lampstand Catholic Reentry Program Model, **(March 25, 2010) E-Report (Free to members only)**

Summary: The purpose of the Lampstand reentry model program is to evangelize criminals--those who are not Catholic and those who are--bringing them the truths of the social teaching of the Church, from a transformed criminal who has become a deep-knowledge leader, as it will lead to the leaving of their criminal life and conversion to communal life. The truths of the Catholic Church trump the truths of the criminal/carceral world, and as important to the criminal--as it is to all men--is the drive to know the truth; which the criminal already thinks he knows and has been living--the truths of the world--taught and learned under the influence of the prince of the world.

St. Dismas Feast Day Policy Primer #5: The
Prison Ministry: A Lampstand Policy Primer,
(March 25, 2011) E-Report (Free to members
only)

Summary: The prison ministry in this policy primer is designed for an individual Catholic parish working with a maximum security prison, through a ministry community of at least four parishioners, in conjunction with the prison's Catholic priest, and supported by prison officials. In order for a Catholic parish to effectively provide a prison ministry that can lead to conversion, a new paradigm in thinking about the criminal world is required rather than the Hollywood dramas or Marxist fantasies too often animating many undertaking this most valuable of ministries called for by Christ in his final teaching to the apostles.

St. Dismas Feast Day Policy Primer #6: The
Criminal's Search for God, Sources, (March 25,
2012) E-Report (Free to members only)

Summary: The collection of source books and the seminal ideas within them, that have played a large role in the development of my thinking—initially to deepen my criminality, but eventually became the soil from which my transformation grew—is a potential transformative tool that can be used as a guide for those criminals seeking to restructure their lives who are not yet prepared to embrace Catholic works. Most of my exploration of the ideas within these books occurred in prison or shortly after release, and as such, they are influences that supported and expanded the underlying narrative of the criminal/carceral world within which I lived and are largely congruent with its driving ethos.

This literature largely emanates from the 1940's to the 1970's—though the ideas are ancient—when the social adulation of the outsider, the outlaw, and the criminal, came into full flower, and it was during the latter decade, that the carceral world was beginning to shape the criminal world.

St. Dismas Feast Day Policy Primer #7: Catholicism, Communism & Criminal Reformation, (March 25, 2013) (Free to members only)

Summary: Communism, and its socialistic method of government, its Marxist method of historical criticism, its violent form of revolution, its state control of religion, and its deep atheism, is a powerful enemy of the Church. We are specifically focusing on Russian Communism, as that is what the Holy Mother of God warned us about at Fatima, and that is the Communism that is the intellectual father of all of the others, deeply engaged since its founding on spreading its revolution worldwide; a revolution that has led, in Russia itself, to the criminal corruption endemic to atheistic governments. The Church has gone from a clear denunciation of Russian Communism by Peter during the 19th and the early 20th century to an accommodation with it immediately prior to and since Vatican II.

St. Dismas Feast Day Policy Primer #8: Women in the Church, Teilhard de Chardin, & Criminal Reformation, (March 25, 2014) (Free to members only)

Summary: The Church stands in the world as a sign of contradiction, and as the world does, and has since time immemorial, excluded women from full personhood, the

Church must ensure that within her embrace, woman's full personhood is deeply rooted and complete; which can only be accomplished by priestly ordination. I have come to believe, fully and completely, that the institutional Church is, and has been, wrong, in not ordaining women to be priests; just as the Church was wrong for centuries in seeing the earth as the center of the solar system, and slavery as acceptable.

Leadership Resources

Resources for Leaders of Criminal Transformation Programs (An annotated listing of professional associations, books, journals, newspapers, websites, reports and other resources for grassroots leaders.) **E-Booklet (Free to members only)**

A Catholic Grassroots Organization Model (A workbook about a model reentry community program, staffed by one transformed criminal, helping 60-70 reentering prisoners annually on an annual budget of $70,000.00) **E-Booklet (Free to members only)**

Annotated Catholic Criminal Justice Bibliography (A resource that can help guide study, research, and reference around the issues that intersect with Catholicism and criminal justice.) **E-Booklet (Free to members only)**

Lampstand Leader's Circle: Definitions, Experiential Requirements, Daily Practice, & Resources (A workbook defining the professional criminals our work is directed to, their life benchmarks, and the daily practice necessary to become a member of the Lampstand Leader's Circle. **E-Booklet (Free to members only)**

Praying the Rosary for the Criminal (A resource that is useful for penitential criminals who pray the rosary, incorporating prayers and brief histories of five great penitential criminal saints: St. Mary Magdalen, St. Dismas, St. Pope Callistus, St. Mary of Egypt, & St. Paul Hanh.) **E-Booklet (Free to members only)**

Periodic Monographs

Lampstand Monograph #1: *Capital Punishment & Matthew 18:6*, **E-Paper (Free to members only)**

Abstract: Matthew 18:6 is perhaps the clearest expression of support for capital punishment spoken by Christ. The Catholic & Protestant commentaries about this verse and the teaching of the entire chapter reveal the vigorous sanctions - capital punishment and banishment - Christ taught as applying to the members of the church community who violate its teachings. Matthew 18 has long been acknowledged as a *Discourse on the Church*, but not enough attention has been devoted to its support for capital punishment; and the historic support of the magisterium for capital punishment, and the corrosive direction taken by some segments of Catholic leadership in the United States to abolish capital punishment, all of which are the subject of this monograph.

Lampstand Monograph #2: *The Way of the Saints & Doing Life*, **E-Paper (Free to members only)**

Abstract: Becoming a true soldier of Christ, fighting to gain entry to heaven, fighting the evil one; this is a call of substance, depth, and honor, which penitential professional criminals imprisoned for life can respond to if the teaching and history of the Church is presented with potency by deeply orthodox Catholics. An unusual cultural aspect of criminal/carceral world culture is the power and influence the elder exerts—almost tribal like in its potency—due to the simple fact that no criminal/prisoner hardly ever retires due to age. I have seen men well into their seventies and eighties who retain the physicality and intellectual heft of men decades younger. The benefits to the criminal/carceral world from the intercessory abilities of a prison saint would be immeasurable.

Chapter Five

There have been several articles published and interviews conducted about Lampstand. Here is a sampling published up to date of publication, (May 2014).

1) These excerpts are from the 2009 article, By the Secret Ladder: Christian Mysticism and Liberation of the Imprisoned, by Dr. Andrew Skotnicki in the journal *Theology Today* (66) 33-44:

In a recent autobiographical account, David Lukenbill writes of the thin line separating the frequently distorted values of penal environments and those in which most of us live: "The cruelty and brutality of the prison is classically evil in the sense that the prisoners are being cruel and brutal consciously. That is the paradigm that works. It is not that there is that much in the prison that doesn't happen on the outside, it's just that in prison it is so much more concentrated." (n. 13, David H. Lukenbill, The Criminal's Search for God (Sacramento, CA: Chulu, 2006), p. 19) (p. 36)

David Lukenbill discovered Thomas Merton in one of his many institutional commitments and similarly writes that there is "much of the monastery in prison." (n. 23, Lukenbill, Criminal's Search for God, p. 18.) Furthermore, he narrates the powerful religious experience he has while on a hunger strike in solitary confinement. In words that recall the self-surrender type of conviction found in the work of William James, he calls it a "break down": "I prayed to God to forgive and protect me and He came to me. I felt such peace and rapture. I felt I was lifted out and walked with Him in a beautiful mountain meadow." (n. 24 Ibid., p. 20.) (pp. 38-39)

2) The following article excerpt is from an interview by Scott Alessi for the In Focus Prison Ministry special in the May 23, 2010 Issue of *Our Sunday Visitor News Weekly.* (pp. 9-12):

Ex-prisoner uses Catholic teaching to break 'criminal world culture'

There's an old adage when dealing with criminals that it takes a thief to catch a thief. But David Lukenbill believes that saying can be taken one step further: It takes a reformed criminal to reform a criminal.

Lukenbill knows firsthand how difficult it can be for a professional criminal to turn his or her life around.

Many years ago, Lukenbill was drawn into a life of crime by the lure of monetary gains, which ultimately landed him inside a maximum security prison. And even though he started to experience some internal rehabilitation during a year in solitary confinement, it didn't hold once he was back among the other inmates.

"Once I got back out into the prison population, I pretty much reverted," Lukenbill said. "The criminal world culture is so dominant in there, and it is pretty hard to counteract that."

3) The following article excerpt is from the January 11, 2011 Catholic Culture website.

Reforming Criminals, By Dr. Jeff Mirus, January 11, 2011

The only daily paper we get in our household is the local paper which covers our town and county in Northern Virginia, or about 375,000 souls. Despite this modest population, nearly every day there is a new local disaster on the front page, very often a crime—burglary, armed robbery, assault, child pornography, even murder. Some of the reports are perversely humorous, as in the recent robbery of a convenience store in which the perpetrator used a six-foot broken branch as a weapon; or the effort to steal a van while the owner was busy in the back. But we've had a string of over twenty burglaries in nearby neighborhoods in recent weeks, there have been some unprovoked gang attacks, and today we learned about the first murder of the new year.

Crimes of passion—and the violent use of an available knife or hand gun in a sudden quarrel—are to some degree understandable, as is the increased incidence of random violence in a crumbling society which is increasingly incapable of nurturing well-adjusted and fundamentally happy people. But consistent criminal activity is a trickier subject; one wonders about the causes that lead someone down that path. A great deal of ink has been spilled over the past fifty years on the sociology of crime, and in particular the degree to which the criminal is himself a victim who cannot be held completely responsible for his actions. Among various attempts to identify root problems, we have seen indictments of society as a whole, of capitalism in particular, and even of the criminal justice system itself.

One man who works directly in this area of assessing criminal responsibility believes that such analyses are fundamentally unproductive. David H. Lukenbill, himself a former 20-year criminal and founder of The Lampstand Foundation, puts the matter succinctly: "In the work of criminal reformation, it is vital to keep in mind that the criminal is the problem." Lukenbill now devotes his life to criminal reformation, and to recruiting other former criminals who have gone on to convert or come back to their Catholic faith (as Lukenbill did) to work directly to touch and transform others.

(4) The following article excerpt is from an interview by Brian Fraga from the June 2012 *US Catholic* magazine.

Crime Fighter

David Lukenbill bears witness to the fact that living outside the law doesn't have to be a life sentence.

A knock on the door introduced David Lukenbill to a life of crime. "My real dad got out of prison when I was 12," recalls Lukenbill. "He showed up on our door one day and my mother said, 'This is your real father'" His dad, a member of the infamous Pendergast gang in Kansas City, Missouri, had spent 10 years behind bars at Fort Leavenworth, Kansas.

Father and son quickly bonded. "I admired my father," says Lukenbill, admitting that he was drawn to his dad's criminal past. Within a couple of years Lukenbill began following in his father's footsteps, stealing and committing armed robberies. He spent 12 of the next 20 years in prison.

"When I was a criminal, I believed that I was acting according to what the truth of the world was," he says. "Rather than working for somebody and enslaving myself for money, I was just taking it, which was what I believed the most powerful people in the world did."

Chapter Six

There have been several articles published in journals by Lampstand, and here is a sampling of articles published up to date of publication, (May 2014).

1) This excerpt is from the book review of Andrew Skotnicki's book *"Criminal Justice and the Catholic Church"* by David H. Lukenbill

Published in the *Journal of Markets & Morality* Volume 11, Number 1, Spring 2008 (pp. 118-119)

Criminal Justice and the Catholic Church
Andrew Skotnicki
Lanham, Maryland: Rowman & Littlefield, 2007
165 pp.

Working in the criminal justice system and having read many of the writings of Andrew Skotnicki, I approached his new book with a certainty that I would be rewarded with well-researched and eloquent expressions of those things which I already agree to be true about an effective criminal justice system, which are: that punishment for crimes is important in a spiritual and temporal sense; that prisons are an appropriate ground for punishment while protecting the public from the criminal in the process; and that the essential impetus for reformation comes from the criminal, not from any external influence applied to him.

There are essentially two criminal justice narratives; one from the academy and many nonprofit advocacy organizations which is primarily sociological and rests on the assumption that we need less of everything involved in criminal justice—crimes, arrests, convictions, prisons—and one from the practitioners (the police, district attorneys, judges and prison guards) who make the case for strengthening the existing system or more of everything.

Dr. Skotnicki's work, as expected from work based on the universal faith of the Catholic Church and her social teaching principles, bridges those two narratives in a way no other perspective can.

2) This excerpt is from a paper published in the *Social Justice Review*, Vol. 100, No. 11-12 November-December, 2009, (pp.150-154)

Catholic Punishment and the Constancy of Catholic Social Teaching, by David H. Lukenbill

The experience of individuals in the world shares certain consistent realities, and among those shared realities is response to institutional constancy. We all share the experience of receiving promises that are not kept, from individuals representing institutions. When this becomes a continual experience, then our response to those promises will often be different than it otherwise would have been. And while we may still embrace the institution, we will become more deeply exasperated by its lack of constancy. While an institution's failure to deliver on promises may merely make some people cynical, it can have disastrous results upon individuals seeking the truth if the institution in question is the Church herself, the custodian of Truth.

When promises are kept and faith is congruent with practice, particularly over a long period of time, constancy is maintained and the level of trust and respect engendered rises proportionately. We have this wonderful gift in our well-informed knowledge of the history of the Church, her great constancy to the ancient truths that are congruent with what she still teaches. Many of these are embodied in the simple, visible movement of the priests and the faithful through the sacraments, but it is in the teaching—built on the stones of Sinai, the ministry, death and resurrection of Christ, and the rock of Peter—that there shines a light in the eternal cathedral of time and memory, embracing us all in the immortal truths.

This constancy is sometimes not easily perceived. The world has attempted to destroy the Church from her very beginning, often with the conscious or unconscious help of her members, and the smoke of Satan's war against the Church has always swirled about the corners of the sanctuary, often as close to us as Cain was to Abel. But the record of the thousand battles of this war during the thousands of years it has been waged, and the great triumphs of Holy Mother Church, are resounding still; even within the darkest heart of a sinner they may resound—and when a penitent soul discovers the mark of this triumph written across the heavens and through the centuries, it can be efficacious in bringing that soul to redemption.

3) This excerpt is from a paper published in the *Social Justice Review*, Vol. 101, No. 11-12 November-December, 2010, (pp.172-175)

The Prison Ministry, by David H. Lukenbill

The prison ministry is one of the most dangerous of ministries but also one of the most valuable. This article will examine the issues involved in developing and sustaining a prison ministry, while making sure that the ministers themselves become proficient and remain protected.

The prison first enters Western consciousness through Genesis and the story of Joseph, sold by his brothers into slavery and became, for a while, a prisoner in Egypt.

Joseph's prison was the "Great Prison," the hnrt wr at Thebes, present-day Luxor, whose existence is unrecorded before the period of the Middle Kingdom. [2050-1786 B.C.] 1

In the New Testament, Christ Himself teaches us to regard visiting those in prison as a work of corporal mercy: "...I was in prison and you came to me." (Matthew 25: 36)

Our prisons have root deriving from Catholic Church history, says Andrew Skotnicki:

My own conclusion is that the prison as we know it in the West originated in the penitential practice of the early church and in primitive monastic communities. With some reservations, I argue that it thus bears a meaning as valid and necessary as penance and monasticism themselves. Perhaps a more restrained way of phrasing it would be that since the contemporary prison is in many ways a Catholic innovation, whatever hope it may have as a locus and vehicle of criminal justice lies within the history we are about to survey. 2

The Catechism of the Catholic Church has more to say about the works of mercy:

The works of mercy are charitable actions by which we come to the aid of our neighbor in his spiritual and bodily necessities. Instructing, advising, consoling, comforting are spiritual works of mercy, as are forgiving and bearing wrongs patiently. The corporal works of mercy consist especially in feeding the hungry, sheltering the homeless, clothing the naked, visiting the sick and imprisoned, and burying the dead. 3

Let us keep in mind the four elements I have just mentioned: the prison as an ancient institution; prison visits as a work of mercy; the prison in the modern West as Catholic- inspired; and works of mercy being how we aid one another. The prison ministry that I present in this article is a spiritual work of mercy directed to prisoners in maximum security prisons, for the purpose of evangelization and the development of transformative criminal/carceral leadership to help other prisoners.

At the end of 2009 there were 1,613,656 prisoners in American federal and state prisons. 4 The population in maximum security prisons hovers around 40% of the total—including the 1-2% in super-maximum security prisons.

In 1974, about 44% of the inmates in state confinement facilities were housed in maximum security prisons; by 2000, this percentage declined to about 38%. 5

The reason for focusing on maximum security prisoners is because they are "the point of the spear", able, if converted, to lead others to conversion. Christ calls us to extend our evangelical reach to the greatest sinners, whose conversion creates the greatest joy in Heaven, revealed in the parable of the prodigal son and in the compassion Christ felt for the two criminal saints, Dismas and Mary of Magdala. Maximum security prisoners are mostly professional criminals—those who commit crimes for money and as a profession—with a strong commitment to the carceral/criminal world, but in the roots of that commitment lies the possibility of a commitment to conversion.

4) This excerpt is from a paper published in the *Social Justice Review*, Vol. 102, No. 11-12 November-December, 2011, (pp.167-171)

The Hierarchy of Evil in the Criminal/Carceral World, by David H. Lukenbill

Within the criminal/carceral world there exists a hierarchy of evil. Professional criminals occupy the upper echelons; informants, rapists and paedophiles occupy the lower. The hierarchy is inverted, as those at the lower end are considered the most evil and those at the top the least evil. This hierarchy plays a crucial rôle for pastoral work related to the rehabilitation or conversion of criminals; the present article examines the hierarchy and its implications for work in the prison ministry.

The work of my apostolate to help reform professional criminals through exposure to the history and social teaching of the Catholic Church can only be as effective as my love for the professional criminal—those who commit crimes for money, and are not informants, paedophiles, or rapists. That love is built on the knowledge of the criminal world that I absorbed during twenty years as a criminal, including twelve years spent in maximum-security state and federal prisons.

Though it has been decades since I was in prison or lived as a criminal among criminals, my love for them continues today, and it manifests itself in the pleasure and joyful anticipation I still feel when I have the opportunity to venture into a maximum-security prison to speak with prisoners. The love I came to know in the criminal/carceral world for professional criminals of both sexes is built upon shared experience and many shared perspectives on the world. It has grown as a result of my deep immersion in Catholicism, which began during the months leading up to my entering the Rite of Christian Initiation for Adults, and has deepened in many ways since my baptism and the founding of the apostolate.

I am no longer a criminal, yet I retain a deep respect and quiet love for some of the cultural artefacts of the criminal/carceral world and the moral principles that have marked criminals since before the criminal saint Dismas hung at Christ's side on Golgotha. This love informs the work of my apostolate—as love of neighbour should always inform the criminal-ministry work undertaken by other Catholics acting in the spirit of the charitable love which Pope Benedict XVI reminds us is at the heart of the Church:

> The Church's deepest nature is expressed in her three-fold responsibility: of proclaiming the word of God (kerygma-martyria), celebrating the sacraments (leitourgia), and exercising the ministry of charity (diakonia). These duties presuppose each other and are inseparable. For the Church, charity is not a kind of welfare activity which could equally well be left to others, but is a part of her nature, an indispensable expression of her very being.1

(p. 167)

About the Author

David H. Lukenbill is a former criminal—thief and robber—who has transformed his life through education—an Associate of Arts degree in Administration of Justice from Sacramento City College, a Bachelor of Science degree in Organizational Behavior from the University of San Francisco, and a Master of Public Administration degree from the University of San Francisco—several years developing, managing, and consulting with criminal transformative organizations, a conversion to Catholicism and a strong marriage and family life.

He is married to his wife of 31 years and they have one child. They live by the American River in California with two cats, and all the wild critters they can feed.

Contact information:

David H. Lukenbill, President
The Lampstand Foundation
Post Office Box 254794
Sacramento, CA 95865-4794

E-mail: Dlukenbill@msn.com

Prayer for Prisoners, Pope Pius XII

O Divine Prisoner of the sanctuary, Who for love of us and for our salvation not only enclosed Yourself within the narrow confines of human nature and then hid Yourself under the veils of the Sacramental Species, but also continually live in the tabernacle! Hear our prayer which rises to You from within these walls and which longs to express to You our affection, our sorrow, and the great need we have of You in our tribulations - above all, in the loss of freedom which so distresses us.

For some of us, there is probably a voice in the depths of conscience which says we are not guilty; that only a tragic judicial error has led us to this prison. In this case, we will draw comfort from remembering that You, the most August of all victims, were also condemned despite Your innocence.

Or perhaps, instead, we must lower our eyes to conceal our blush of shame, and beat our breast. But, even so, we also have the remedy of throwing ourselves into Your arms, certain that You understand all errors, forgive all sins, and generously restore Your grace to him who turns to You in repentance.

And finally, there are those among us who have succumbed to sin so often through the course of our earthly lives that even the best among men mistrust us, and we ourselves hardly know how to set out on the new road of regeneration. But despite all this, in the most hidden corner of our soul a voice of trust and comfort whispers Your words, promising us the help of Your light and Your grace if we want to return to what is good.

May we, 0 Lord, never forget that the day of trial is an opportune time for purifying the spirit, practicing the highest virtues, and acquiring the greatest merits. Let not our afflicted hearts be affected by that disgust which dries up everything, or by that distrust which leaves no room for brotherly sentiments and which prepared the road for bad counsel. May we always remember that, in depriving us of the freedom of our bodies, no one has been able to deprive us of freedom of the soul, which during the long hours of our solitude can rise to You to know You better and love You more each day.

Grant, 0 Divine Savior, help and resignation to the dear ones who mourn our absence. Grant peace and quiet to this world which has rejected us but which we love and to which we promise our co-operation as good citizens for the future.

Grant that our sorrows may be a salutary example to many souls and that they may thus be protected against the dangers of following our path. But above all, grant us the grace of believing firmly in You, of filially hoping in You, and of loving You: Who, with the Father and the Holy Spirit, live and reign forever and ever.

Amen.

O Sacred Heart of Jesus, make us love Thee more and more!
Our Lady of Hope, pray for us!
Saint Dismas, the Good Thief, pray for us!

Pius XII, April 1958

Prayer to St. Dismas

Glorious Saint Dismas, you alone of all the great Penitent Saints were directly canonized by Christ Himself; you were assured of a place in Heaven with Him "*this day*" because of the sincere confession of your sins to Him in the tribunal of Calvary and your true sorrow for them as you hung beside Him in that open confessional; you who by your love and repentance did open the Heart of Jesus in mercy and forgiveness even before the centurion's spear tore it asunder; you whose face was closer to that of Jesus in His last agony, to offer Him a word of comfort, closer even than that of His Beloved Mother, Mary; you who knew so well how to pray, teach me the words to say to Him to gain pardon and the grace of perseverance; and you who are so close to Him now in Heaven, as you were during His last moments on earth, pray to Him for me that I shall never again desert Him, but that at the close of my life I may hear from Him the words He addressed to you: "This day thou shalt be with Me in Paradise." Amen.

Prayer to St. Michael for Protection of the Catholic Church and Her Members

✠ **Glorious St. Michael,** Guardian and Defender of the Church of Jesus Christ, come to the assistance of the Church, against which the powers of Hell are unchained. Guard with thy special care her august visible head, and obtain for him and for us that the hour of triumph may speedily arrive.

✠ **Glorious Archangel St. Michael,** watch over us during life, defend us against the assaults of the demon, assist us especially at the hour of death, obtain for us a favorable judgment and the happiness of beholding God face to face for endless ages. Amen

www.ingramcontent.com/pod-product-compliance
Lightning Source LLC
La Vergne TN
LVHW021548080426
835509LV00019B/2900